onelove

onelove

Photography by Levon Biss
Foreword by Steve Rushin

UNIVERSE

THE AIM

of the *One Love* project was to document the game of football in its entirety, from small children playing in the mountains of Peru to professionals playing at the pinnacle of the game for their country. For me, the vendor selling burgers outside a stadium is just as much a part of football culture as the player on the pitch—and it was from this viewpoint that I began the photography.

The *One Love* project covers twenty-six countries and shows a cross section of diverse cultures brought together by the commonality of football—the world's only truly global sport. Along the way I saw grown men cry like babies, and disabled children play with courage beyond their years. To this day, the influence of football continues to surprise, inspire, and humble me in equal measure.

One of my favorite memories from the project was in Buenos Aires at the derby between Boca Juniors and River Plate. The intensity, passion, and raw emotion of the rival supporters was so great, I could not take my eyes off them. In fact, I think I only watched about five minutes of football during the entire game!

Through the imagery within this book, I have been able to share these amazing experiences and scenes with a much wider audience.

With the generous support of UMBRO International and their licensees from around the world, the assistance of Apple Computers and RPM London, the *One Love* project is now a reality. The confidence, enthusiasm, and dedication they have shown to this project turned a dream into a reality.

Thank you.
Levon Biss
London, January 2006

ONE LOVE

The image on the cover of this book, of a man who appears literally to have the world at his feet, calls to mind the lyrics of the English band XTC, who sang, "All the world is football-shaped. It's just for me to kick in space." But the title of *One Love* is inspired by another football-obsessed musician, Bob Marley, who said at various times that "Football is music," and "Football is freedom," and "Football is a part of I: when I play, the world wakes up around me."

The pages that follow are alive with music and freedom. (Witness the pitch invasion on page 151, as supporters giddily pour over a wall like prison lifers on the lam.) Between these covers, the world wakes up around us, as in one of those time-lapse films of a flower blooming, entire days contained in the span of a single minute. Here, in a few pages, is the planet: beaches, back alleys, deserts, donkey carts, pubs, police dogs, and a lone penalty spot, spray-painted in snow. It is a world atlas worthy of Atlas, if only he had had enough sense to dribble the Earth at his feet, not hump it around on his shoulders.

Some years ago, in a remote village of remote Greenland at 3 o'clock on a moonless morning, I found myself on a narrow street echoing with that other song of world harmony—not "One Love" but "Kumbaya," the hippie hand-holder whose lyrics had been modified to honor a Manchester United midfielder who had scored twice that day. As members of a motley, multinational group of Greenlanders and tourists left a house party, they sang: *"He scores goals galore, he scores goals/He scores goals galore, he scores goals/He scores goals galore, he scores goals. Paul Scho-oles, he scores goals."*

At that moment—at the top of the globe, in the Arctic Circle—I really did have the world at my feet. And it certainly looked football-shaped to me.

Steve Rushin
2006

7

SOME PEOPLE BELIEVE
FOOTBALL IS A MATTER OF LIFE
AND DEATH. I'M VERY
DISAPPOINTED WITH THAT
ATTITUDE. I CAN ASSURE YOU IT
IS MUCH, MUCH MORE
IMPORTANT THAN
THAT. – BILL SHANKLY

AWAY SUPPORTERS' FLAGS
AT A J-LEAGUE GAME, OSAKA,
JAPAN.

»» ONE OF THE GROUND STAFF
AT THE BLACK LEOPARDS'
STADIUM PREPARES THE PITCH
BEFORE A GAME AGAINST THE
BUSH BUCKS IN MAKHADO,
SOUTH AFRICA.

»»» A GROUNDSPERSON AT THE
TRAINING FACILITIES OF
SHANGHAI SHENUA FC,
SHANGHAI, CHINA.

I WORSHIP THE DRIBBLE. AS A CHILD I DID NOTHING BUT DRIBBLE. IN THE LIVING ROOM, BETWEEN THE FURNITURE AND THE CHAIRS, IN THE GARDEN AROUND MY DOG. I LEARNED ALL ABOUT LIFE WITH THE BALL AT MY FEET. – RONALDINHO

FOOTBALL MEANS FREEDOM.
– BOB MARLEY

GEM SELLERS PLAY ON THE SIDE OF A ROAD IN NAMIBIA. THE MEN SELL SEMI-PRECIOUS STONES TO PASSING TRAFFIC BUT WITH BUSINESS SCARCE, THEY PLAY FOOTBALL TO PASS THE TIME.

›› PUCA PUCARA VILLAGERS PLAYING NEAR CUZCO, PERU.

›››› PAKISTANI CONSTRUCTION WORKERS TAKE A BREAK ON THE HATTA ROAD, DUBAI.

IT COULDN'T BE EASIER TO
START A REVOLUTION IN
FRANCE: JUST TAKE FOOTBALL
OFF THE TELEVISION AND
EVERYONE WILL POUR
ONTO THE STREETS.
– JEAN-LUC GODARD

BLACK LEOPARDS PLAYERS PRAY BEFORE A GAME, MAKHAGO, SOUTH AFRICA.

›› GEM SELLERS WALK HOME TO THEIR SETTLEMENT, ERANGOU, NAMIBIA.

›››› LOCAL FOOTBALL IN PINERY PARK, TORONTO, CANADA.

I WILL WRITE MY LIFE AS IF IT WERE A LOVE STORY, FOR WHO SHALL SAY IT IS NOT? IT BEGAN WITH MY GREAT LOVE OF FOOTBALL AND IT WILL END THE SAME. – FERENC PUSKAS

TABLE FOOTBALL AT ATTICA FOOTBALL PARK, ATHENS, GREECE.

›› MACHEKOANENG, LESOTHO.

›››› WEEKEND GAMES IN COSTANERA, BUENOS AIRES, ARGENTINA.

FACTORY WORKERS PLAYING
AFTER THEIR SHIFT, MASERU,
LESOTHO.

›› WORKERS AT A LIME QUARRY
AT ULUWATU, BALI, INDONESIA.

›››› MAURI CHILDREN PLAYING
IN THEIR BACK GARDEN,
WHAKAREWAREWA,
NEW ZEALAND.

BLACK OR WHITE, WE ALL HAVE FOOTBALL UNDER OUR SKIN. – EUSEBIO

IF YOU ARE IN THE PENALTY AREA AND YOU DON'T KNOW WHAT TO DO WITH THE BALL, PUT IT IN THE NET AND WE'LL DISCUSS THE OPTIONS LATER. – BOB PAISLEY

PUTTING THE NETS UP BEFORE A SUNDAY LEAGUE GAME ON HACKNEY MARSHES, LONDON, ENGLAND.

›› MACHEKOANENG, LESOTHO.

›››› TEENAGERS AT TAMAN UJUNG GARDENS, BALI, INDONESIA.

FOOTBALL IS NOT FOR BALLERINAS. – CLAUDIO GENTILE

AN OFFICE WORKER DURING A FRIENDLY MATCH HELD IN THE EVENING AT BURNS PARK, MASSAPEQUA, USA.

›› BORACIA BEACH, SAO PAULO, BRAZIL.

›››› SHANGHAI SHENUA FC, SHANGHAI, CHINA.

THROUGH THE
TURNSTILE INTO
ANOTHER AND ALTOGETHER
MORE SPLENDID KIND
OF LIFE, HURTLING
WITH CONFLICT AND
YET PASSIONATE AND
BEAUTIFUL IN ITS ART.
– J. B. PRIESTLY

AN ATLÉTICO PARANAENSE
SUPPORTER SHOUTS TO HIS
TEAM DURING A MATCH AT VILA
BELMIRO, SANTOS, BRAZIL.

›› A TRADER ARGUES WITH
SOLDIERS BEFORE A MATCH,
MOSCOW, RUSSIA.

›››› CHINESE POLICE SIT AND
WAIT FOR THE ARRIVAL OF THE
FANS AT A FIRST DIVISION
GAME, SHANGHAI, CHINA.

I AM BOTH BLACK AND WHITE. I AM SOMETHING IN BETWEEN – I LOVE BOTH AND COULD NEVER CHOOSE BETWEEN THE TWO. – MARCEL DESAILLY

J-LEAGUE GAME, OSAKA, JAPAN.

›› PUCA PUCAR, NEAR CUZCO, PERU.

›››› AN IRISH FAN WEARS HIS LUCKY HAT AT AN INTERNATIONAL MATCH, DUBLIN, IRELAND.

ULBRA UNIVERSITY, PORTO ALE-
GRE, BRAZIL.

›› CHILDREN PLAYING IN THE
VILLAGE OF PISAC, PERU.

›››› LUIS GARCIA OF LIVERPOOL
FC IN HIS OFFICE AT HOME IN
LIVERPOOL, ENGLAND.
THE PICTURE ON THE WALL
SHOWS HIM POISED FOR THE
WINNING SHOT IN THE
CHAMPIONS LEAGUE FINAL IN
2005.

FOOTBALL IS THE BEAUTIFUL GAME.
– PELÉ

THE LONG WAIT FOR THE NEXT GAME AT THE UMBRO INTERNATIONAL YOUTH CUP, MANCHESTER, ENGLAND.

PLAYERS DON'T WIN TROPHIES – TEAMS WIN TROPHIES. – JOSE MOURINHO

›› "KEEP OFF THE GRASS!" SHANGHAI, CHINA.

›››› SATURDAY MORNING AT THE SIDE OF THE YODO RIVER IN THE FUKUSHIMA DISTRICT OF OSAKA, JAPAN.

ONE BALL IS ENOUGH
FOR ALL, AND IF
THERE'S SPACE, ALL
YOU NEED IS ENTHUSIASM.
– JORGE VALDANO

NEW YORK, USA.

›› BARCELONA, SPAIN.

›››› URBAN PITCHES, LIMA,
PERU.

THERE'S ONLY ONE POSSIBILITY: WIN, DRAW, OR LOSE.

CHINESE FANS LOOK ON ANXIOUSLY AFTER THEIR TEAM IS AWARDED A PENALTY IN THE LAST MINUTE OF THE GAME, SHANGHAI, CHINA.

– FRANZ BECKENBAUER

›› **HAN-NAN UNIVERSITY, OSAKA, JAPAN.**

››› **A MAN AND HIS BOYS PLAY IN A RURAL VILLAGE, PERU.**

THERE'S NO CHILDHOOD MORE DELIGHTFUL THAN ONE POISED BETWEEN SPORT AND IMAGINATION. – ERIC CANTONA

›› CAR PARK ATTENDANT AT ELLAND ROAD FOOTBALL GROUND, LEEDS, ENGLAND.

›››› DANUBIO VERSUS RIVER PLATE AT PARQUE R. SAROLDI STADIUM, MONTEVIDEO, URUGUAY.

THERE HAS TO BE
THOUGHT BEHIND
EVERY TOUCH OF THE BALL.
– DENNIS BERGKAMP

TO THE AESTHETE IT IS AN ART FORM, AN ATHLETIC BALLET. TO THE SPIRITUALLY INCLINED IT IS A RELIGION.
– PAUL GARDNER

A SOCCER GAME WITHOUT GOALS IS LIKE AN AFTERNOON WITHOUT SUNSHINE.

– ALFREDO DI STEFANO

>> SANTOS SUPPORTERS DURING A GAME AGAINST ATLÉTICO PARANAENSE AT VILA BELMIRO, SANTOS, BRAZIL.

>>>> JUNIOR TEAMS POSE FOR A PICTURE AFTER A CUP FINAL, OSAKA, JAPAN.

IF YOU MAKE FOOTBALL TOO IMPORTANT YOU DEPRIVE IT OF ITS BEAUTY. AFRICANS PLAY PURE STREET FOOTBALL. FOOTBALL IS A GAME OF FUN! – KANU

WOMEN'S OVER-65 FOOTBALL AT THOHOYANDOU UNIVERSITY, SOUTH AFRICA. AS PART OF A LOCAL GOVERNMENT SCHEME TO PROMOTE HEALTHY LIVING AMONG THE ELDERLY, LOCAL TRIBES HAVE FORMED TEAMS AND PLAY REGULARLY IN LEAGUES.

» SANTOS FANS CELEBRATE A GOAL AGAINST ATLÉTICO PARANAENSE AT THE VILA BELMIRO, SANTOS, BRAZIL.

»»» A SOLDIER REMOVES A FLARE FROM THE CROWD DURING A GAME, SHANGHAI, CHINA.

SHANGHAI SHENUA FC,
SHANGHAI, CHINA.

›› SAN GAO FOOTBALL SCHOOL,
BEIJING, CHINA.

›››› SCHOOL KIDS PLAY ON A
DIRT PITCH UNDER PYLONS IN
ORLANDO EAST, SOWETO,
SOUTH AFRICA.

THE BALL IS MADE ROUND TO GO ROUND. — MATT BUSBY

BEACH SOCCER ON VIRGINIA BEACH, VIRGINIA, USA.

THE FAMOUS BICICLETA OR BICYCLE KICK. IT WAS DEVELOPED BY LEONIDAS DA SILVA, A VERY FAMOUS BRAZILIAN PLAYER IN THE WORLD CUP OF 1938. THE KICK IS EXECUTED BY THROWING YOUR BODY IN THE AIR, HORIZONTALLY, WITH THE SHOOTING LEG BENT AT THE KNEE. THEN, JUST AS THE BALL APPROACHES, THIS LEG IS STRAIGHTENED UP TO PROPEL THE BALL BACKWARD, OVER THE HEAD. THE HANDS ARE SPREAD TO CUSHION THE FALL, AND THE PLAY IS FINISHED. EVERY BRAZILIAN FOOTBALL PLAYER LONGS FOR THE OPPORTUNITY TO PERFORM THIS KICK, IF ONLY FOR THE PLEASURE OF THE FANS. – PELÉ

» SHIGA MORIYAMA, JAPAN.

»»» KIDS PLAYING IN LAOU SQUARE IN THE NEIGHBOR-HOOD OF KERATSINI, ATHENS, GREECE.

WHAT IT'S ALL ABOUT IS CHILDREN ENJOYING FOOTBALL AND NOT FINDING IT A CHORE. SO THE BEST WAY TO TEACH A CHILD TO PLAY FOOTBALL IS TO ENCOURAGE, NOT SUPPRESS. — JOHAN CRUYFF

SUCCESS IS NO ACCIDENT. IT IS HARD WORK, PERSEVERANCE, LEARNING, STUDYING, SACRIFICE, AND MOST OF ALL, LOVE OF WHAT YOU ARE DOING OR LEARNING TO DO. – PELÉ

TRAINING AT ULBRA UNIVER-SITY, PORTO ALEGRE, BRAZIL.

›› FOOT VOLLEYBALL ON COPACABANA BEACH, RIO DE JANEIRO, BRAZIL.

›››› TEAM MASCOTS WAIT FOR THE PLAYERS IN THE TUNNEL AT OLYMPIC LYONNAIS, LYON, FRANCE.

I EAT FOOTBALL,
I SLEEP FOOTBALL,
I BREATHE FOOTBALL.
I'M NOT MAD, I'M JUST
PASSIONATE. – THIERRY HENRY

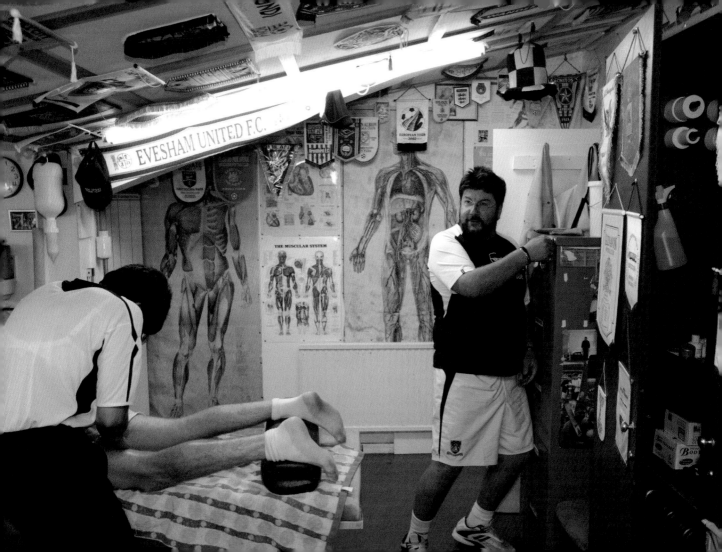

THE IMAGINED COMMUNITY OF MILLIONS SEEMS MORE REAL AS A TEAM OF ELEVEN NAMED PEOPLE.
– ERIC HOBSBAWM

THE MOST IMPORTANT THING TO US WAS OUR FREEDOM. AND IT WAS MY GRANDMOTHER WHO GAVE ME THIS FREEDOM. BECAUSE MY GRANDMOTHER ALLOWED US TO GO OUT, TO DO WHAT WE WANTED, AND ABOVE ALL TO PLAY FOOTBALL. – GEORGE WEAH

PLAYING IN THE BACK GARDEN, NORWAY.

›› BEACH SOCCER ON VIRGINIA BEACH, VIRGINIA, USA.

›››› DAILY TRAINING AT THE SAN GAO FOOTBALL SCHOOL, BEIJING, CHINA. THE SCHOOL HAS OVER 500 PUPILS WHO STUDY TRADITIONAL SUBJECTS IN THE MORNING AND FOOTBALL IN THE AFTERNOON.

FOOTBALL HAS BECOME BRAZIL'S GREATEST LEVELLER.
– MARIO FILHO

JARDIM MIRIAM COMMUNITY
PITCH, SAO PAULO, BRAZIL.

›› A GAME PLAYED IN FRONT OF
PONDOKS ROCKS, SPITZKOPPE,
NAMIBIA.

›››› SHANGHAI, CHINA.

THE SOCIALISM I BELIEVE IN IS EVERYONE WORKING FOR EACH OTHER, EVERYONE HAVING A SHARE OF THE REWARDS. IT'S THE WAY I SEE FOOTBALL, THE WAY I SEE LIFE. – BILL SHANKLY

SANTOS FANS OUTSIDE THE VILA BELMIRO STADIUM, SANTOS, BRAZIL.

›› A GROUNDSMAN'S HANDS ARE STAINED WITH WHITE LIME POWDER AFTER MARKING THE LINES OF A PITCH, HAMUTSHA, SOUTH AFRICA.

›››› PAINTING THE LINES OF A PITCH BEFORE A GAME, HAMUTSHA, SOUTH AFRICA.

STREET FOOTBALL WAS AND IS THE BEST NATURAL WAY OF TRAINING YOU CAN FIND. IT GIVES A BETTER FEELING FOR THE GAME. – RINUS MICHELS

PLAYERS FROM THE JAPANESE TEAM WARM UP BEFORE A GAME AGAINST PORTUGAL IN THE HOMELESS WORLD CUP, GOTHENBURG, SWEDEN.

›› SEATS ARE CLEANED AT CD ESPANYOL IN PREPARATION FOR THE EVENING GAME, BARCELONA, SPAIN.

›››› A SUPPORTER WALKS HOME AFTER THE FINAL OF THE HOMELESS WORLD CUP, GOTHENBURG, SWEDEN.

I'M SURE SEX WOULDN'T BE AS REWARDING AS WINNING THE WORLD CUP. IT'S NOT THAT SEX ISN'T GOOD, BUT THE WORLD CUP IS EVERY FOUR YEARS AND SEX IS NOT.
– RONALDO

SINGING FANS MAKE THEIR WAY THROUGH THE STADIUM BEFORE A GAME BETWEEN THE MORROKA SWALLOWS AND THE KAISER CHIEFS, JOHANNESBURG, SOUTH AFRICA.

» CHELSEA CAPTAIN AND ENGLAND INTERNATIONAL JOHN TERRY RELAXING AT HIS HOME, LONDON, ENGLAND.

»» MICHAEL OWEN OF NEWCASTLE AND ENGLAND TRAINS IN THE GYM WHILE RECOVERING FROM A BROKEN FOOT.

AS LONG AS THE HUMAN RACE IS ABLE TO CONCERN ITSELF WITH MORE THAN MERE SURVIVAL, SOCCER WILL HAVE ITS PLACE.
– DESMOND MORRIS

AN ARGENTINIAN PLAYER WARMS UP AT THE HOMELESS WORLD CUP, GOTHENBURG, SWEDEN.

›› KIDS PLAY ON A PITCH DUG OUT OF THE GROUND, DUTHUNI, SOUTH AFRICA.

›››› URUGUAY NATIONAL BEACH SOCCER TEAM, TRAINING ON MONTEVIDEO BEACH, URUGUAY.

LIFE ITSELF IS BUT A GAME OF FOOTBALL.
– SIR WALTER SCOTT

A LOCAL MATCH BEGINS IN PETROVSKIY, A REMOTE RURAL TOWN 150 KILOMETERS FROM MOSCOW, RUSSIA.

›› A GAME IN THE ERANGOU SETTLEMENT, NAMIBIA.

›››› FELTHAM FOOTBALL FESTIVAL, LONDON, ENGLAND.

IN THE DRESSING ROOM IT DOESN'T MATTER IF YOU ARE BLACK, WHITE, JEWISH, CHRISTIAN, OR MUSLIM. ALL THAT MATTERS IS THAT YOU CAN KICK A BALL AND HAVE A GOOD LAUGH WITH EACH OTHER.
– MOHAMMED ALLACH

BLACK LEOPARDS FORWARD MULONDO SIKHWIVHILU LACES HIS BOOTS BEFORE A GAME IN HIS BEDROOM AT THE TEAM'S COMMUNAL HOUSE, MAKHADO, SOUTH AFRICA.

›› MORECAMBE TOWN FOOTBALL CLUB, MORECAMBE, ENGLAND.

›››› BEACH SOCCER ON COPACABANA BEACH, RIO DE JANEIRO, BRAZIL.

FOOTBALL IS A
SIMPLE GAME MADE
COMPLICATED BY
PEOPLE WHO SHOULD
KNOW BETTER. – BILL SHANKLY

GROUNDSMAN AT UNIVERSI-
TARIO DE DEPORTES STADIUM,
AREQUIPA, PERU.

»»» AN EMPTY GOAL IN A
BARREN LANDSCAPE OF THE
NADALSHEBA DISTRICT ON THE
OUTSKIRTS OF DUBAI.

»» AN EMPTY GOAL, BAJADA
MARBELLA, PERU.

THERE IS A DEEP CONNECTION BETWEEN TRICKING DEFENDERS AND BEING A SMART BOY IN REAL LIFE. — SIMON KUPER

EVERYTHING I KNOW ABOUT FOOTBALL I LEARNED ON THE STREET. MY FRIENDS AND I WERE ALWAYS TRYING TO THINK UP A NEW FEINT. IF ANYONE INVENTED SOMETHING NEW, THEY HAD TO SHOW IT TO THE OTHERS. THAT IS WHAT STREET FOOTBALL IS ALL ABOUT.
– ZINÉDINE ZIDANE

FOOTBALL IS THE BALLET OF THE MASSES.
– DMITRI SHOSTAKOVICH

PITCH INVASION BY WILLEM II FANS AFTER AN UNEXPECTED VICTORY OVER AJAX, TILBURG, HOLLAND.

›› HOTEL WORKERS PLAY A GAME AFTER WORK NEAR AYERS ROCK, AUSTRALIA.

›››› A MAN PLAYS AGAINST A WALL IN A HU TONG CALLED GU LOU, BEIJING, CHINA.

I PLAY FOOTBALL FOR THE PEOPLE. THE MAN WHO STANDS IN THE

FACTORY ALL WEEK OR DOES BORING WORK AT THE OFFICE, THE SCHOOL PUPIL OVERLOADED WITH HOMEWORK, PEOPLE WHO HAVE LOST THEIR JOBS, MEN AND WOMEN WHO HAVE IT HARD. – WILLEM VAN HANEGEM

A PENALTY IS A COWARDLY WAY TO SCORE. – PELÉ

MARKING THE PENALTY SPOT BEFORE AN EVENING GAME, NORTHERN NORWAY. THE TEMPERATURE IS -18 DEGREES AND THE PITCH IS MADE OF ICE.

» A SUNDAY AFTERNOON, LOCAL LEAGUE MATCH PLAYED ON A RED DIRT PITCH, THOHOYANDOU, SOUTH AFRICA.

»» MORIYAMAKITA HIGH SCHOOL, THREE HOURS NORTH-EAST OF OSAKA, JAPAN.

FOOTBALL IS THE UNIVERSAL GAME OF ALL CHILDREN. –LILIAN THURAM

CLIMATE, TEMPERATURE, HISTORY – ALL THESE CONTRIBUTE TO STYLE, WHICH IS AN ASPECT OF CHARACTER, INDIVIDUAL OR NATIONAL.

URUGUAY NATIONAL BEACH SOCCER TEAM, TRAINING ON MONTEVIDEO BEACH, URUGUAY.

›› HARD-CORE SUPPORTERS OF GAMBA OSAKA WAIT OUTSIDE THE GROUND FOR THE GAME TO BEGIN, OSAKA, JAPAN.

›››› SANTOS FANS, SANTOS, BRAZIL.

– OFFICIAL FOOTBALL ASSOCIATION YEARBOOK

WHEN OUR NATIONAL TEAM PLAYS, WE FEEL THAT THE IDENTITY OF OUR COUNTRY IS BEING PLAYED OUT ON THE FIELD.
– LUIS EDUARDO SOARES

TICKET TOUTS OUTSIDE THE GROUND, SELLING TICKETS FOR THE LAST GAME OF THE SEASON AT SHANGHAI SHENUA FC, SHANGHAI, CHINA. TICKETS BOUGHT ON THE STREET FOR THIS GAME WERE SOLD AT THREE TIMES THE NORMAL PRICE.

HAPPINESS IS NOT BEING AFRAID.

– ROY KEANE

THE JOY OF SEEING YURI GAGARIN FLYING IN SPACE IS ONLY SUPERSEDED BY THE JOY OF A GOOD PENALTY SAVE. – LEV YASHIN

GOALKEEPERS, MATSUBARA, JAPAN.

I WAS BORN IN FOOTBALL.
FOOTBALL IS A FANTASTIC AND
INTELLIGENT GAME
WHICH TEACHES US
HOW TO LIVE TOGETHER,
HOW TO SHARE WHEN
YOU ARE BETTER THAN
OTHERS. FOOTBALL IS AN
EXTRAORDINARY EDUCATION FOR
LIFE. – MICHEL PLATINI

BOYS PLAYING IN THE BACKSTREETS OF MONASTI-RAKI, ATHENS, GREECE.

›› TEENAGERS PLAYING AFTER SCHOOL IN A STREET MARKET, DUTHUNI, SOUTH AFRICA.

›››› MORECAMBE TOWN FOOTBALL CLUB, MORECAMBE, ENGLAND.

SOCCER IS OFTEN MORE
DEEPLY FELT THAN
RELIGION, AND JUST AS MUCH
A PART OF THE COMMUNITY'S
FABRIC, A REPOSITORY OF
TRADITIONS. – FRANKLIN FOER

THE FIRST 90 MINUTES ARE THE MOST IMPORTANT. – BOBBY ROBSON

FOOTBALL IS SIMPLE. BUT THE HARDEST THING IS TO PLAY FOOTBALL IN A SIMPLE WAY. –JOHAN CRUYFF

185

THE SPEED I DON'T POSSESS IN MY LEGS, I HAVE IN MY HEAD.
– DAVID TREZEGUET

SOCCER WAS INVENTED BY A MAN BUT PERFECTED BY A WOMAN.

– JULIE FOUDY

IF THERE WEREN'T SUCH A THING AS FOOTBALL, WE'D ALL BE FRUSTRATED FOOTBALLERS.

– MICK LYONS

195

I'M MARRIED TO FOOTBALL AND HAVE AN AFFAIR WITH MY WIFE.

– BOBBY ROBSON

AN IMPROMPTU NIGHT MATCH AT RENON FIELDS IN DEN-PASAR, BALI, INDONESIA.

›› PRAMBARAN TEMPLE ON THE BORDER OF MIDDLE JAVA AND JOGJAKARTA, INDONESIA.

›››› RED SQUARE, MOSCOW, RUSSIA.

WHAT KIND OF GAME IS THIS – DEMONIC AND DIVINE?
– MARGUERITE DURAS

SEX BEFORE THE GAME? THAT'S FOR THE PLAYERS TO DECIDE, BUT IT'S UNACCEPTABLE DURING THE HALF-TIME BREAK. – BERTI VOGTS

MISS BLACK LEOPARDS IS INTERVIEWED AT HALF-TIME DURING A GAME AGAINST THE BUSH BUCKS, MAKHADO, SOUTH AFRICA.

THE ACT OF PLAYING FOR THE TEAM MAKES EVERY INDIVIDUAL STRONGER.
– ARSENE WENGER

TRAINING SESSION AT THE
TSUMORI GROUND, OSAKA,
JAPAN.

›› GAMBA OSAKA SUPPORTERS
WAIT FOR THE START OF THE
GAME, OSAKA, JAPAN.

›››› SPARTAK SUPPORTERS
CELEBRATE, MOSCOW, RUSSIA.

FOOTBALL IS A GAME. FOR ME, PLEASURE ALWAYS COMES FIRST. – THIERRY HENRY

A PERSONALIZED FOOTBALL SHIRT, DUTHUNI, SOUTH AFRICA.

TWO THINGS ARE CERTAIN IN LIFE. PEOPLE DIE AND COACHES GET SACKED. –AAD DE MOS

THE TEAM MASCOT TAKES A WELL-DESERVED REST FROM ENTERTAINING THE CROWD AFTER A MATCH, ATLANTA, USA.

›› TABLE FOOTBALL IN AN INFORMAL SETTLEMENT CALLED MOTSOALEDI, SOWETO, SOUTH AFRICA.

›››› TABLE FOOTBALL OUTSIDE A CORNER SHOP IN BARRIO SAAVEDRA, BUENOS AIRES, ARGENTINA.

FOOTBALL IS ALL VERY WELL AS A GAME FOR ROUGH GIRLS, BUT IT IS HARDLY SUITABLE FOR DELICATE BOYS.
– OSCAR WILDE

FOOTBALL IS THE OPERA OF THE PEOPLE.
—STAFFORD HEGINBOTTOM

SOCCER IS SIMPLE... YOU JUST NEED TO HAVE THE RIGHT MENTALITY, FIGHTING IN EVERY GAME, IN EVERY PRACTICE AND FOR EVERY BALL.
– HRISTO STOICHKOV

EVERY TIME I WENT OUT I WAS
DECEIVING MY MUM.
I'D TELL HER I WAS
GOING TO SCHOOL BUT
I'D BE OUT ON THE
STREET PLAYING FOOTBALL.
– RONALDO

FOOTBALL CAN MAKE A SMALL COUNTRY BIG.

– ROGER MILLA

LIFE GETS COMPLICATED WHEN YOU LOVE ONE WOMAN AND WORSHIP ELEVEN MEN.
– NICK HORNBY

THE BEST REFEREE HAS GOOD EYES AND BAD HEARING. – MARIO VAN ENDE

MANCHESTER, ENGLAND.

›› DUSTY FOOTBALLS AFTER PRACTICE AT THE SAN GAO FOOTBALL SCHOOL, BEIJING, CHINA.

›››› FUTSAL IN AN OLD GYM, PORTO, PORTUGAL.

THERE IS ALWAYS THE DREAM. IT IS THAT YOU WILL CONQUER YOUR FEARS, AND WHEN IT MATTERS MOST YOU WILL FIND POWER YOU NEVER HAD BEFORE. – RONALDO

HAN-NAN UNIVERSITY, OSAKA, JAPAN.

›› SHADOWS OF SUPPORTERS AT AN IRELAND VERSUS FRANCE UNDER-21 MATCH, CORK, IRELAND.

›››› OAKVILLE SC VERSUS SALTFLEET SC IN A BOYS' UNDER-11 GAME, TORONTO, CANADA.

YOU DON'T STOP PLAYING FOOTBALL BECAUSE YOU GET OLD, YOU GET OLD BECAUSE YOU STOP PLAYING FOOTBALL. — STANLEY MATTHEWS

GAUCHOS AT THE SANTA SUSANA RANCH, LOS CARDALES, ARGENTINA.

›› GRASSROOTS FOOTBALL, MONTEVIDEO, URUGUAY.

›››› ONLY FRIENDS, A DISABLED CHILDREN'S FOOTBALL CLUB, AMSTERDAM, HOLLAND.

THERE IS NO GREATER DRAMA IN SPORT THAN A SOCCER TEAM TRYING TO VALIDATE ITS NATIONAL CHARACTER IN THE WORLD CUP. – JEFF RUSNAK

THE ENGLAND UNDER-21 TEAM BUS LEAVES THE HOTEL BEFORE A WORLD CUP QUALIFIER AGAINST AUSTRIA, LEEDS, ENGLAND.

EVERY DEFEAT IS A VICTORY IN ITSELF.
– FRANCISCO MATURANA

PENAROL FC, MONTEVIDEO,
URUGUAY.

≫ CHEERLEADERS WAIT
BEFORE A MATCH,
MORECAMBE, ENGLAND.

≫≫ JAPANESE PLAYERS WAIT
FOR THEIR NEXT GAME AT THE
HOMELESS WORLD CUP,
GOTHENBURG, SWEDEN.

THE WORLD CUP IS... FOR THE ESTIMATED TWO BILLION VIEWERS WHO GET UP EARLY, STAY UP LATE, CHEER AT THE TELEVISION, BAY AT THE MOON, GO OUT AND BANG DRUMS IN THE MIDDLE OF THE NIGHT BECAUSE SOMEBODY SCORED A GOAL HALFWAY AROUND THE WORLD. – GEORGE VESCEY

SUPPORTERS OF ANTWERP FC WATCH A GAME AGAINST ROESELARE, ANTWERP, BELGIUM.

THE WORLD OF FOOTBALL IS DIFFERENT FROM THE WORLD OF POLITICS.
– DARIUSH MOSTOFAVI

REFEREES PREPARE THEIR CARDS BEFORE A GAME, MORECAMBE, ENGLAND.

›› BEACH SOCCER TOURNAMENT, FUERTEVENTURA, SPAIN.

›››› A REFEREE MARKS THE FINAL SCORE FOR THE LOCAL NEWSPAPER'S PHOTOGRAPHER, THOHOYANDOU, SOUTH AFRICA.

FOOTBALL IS A SIMPLE GAME MADE DIFFICULT BY THE PLAYERS.

PLAYERS PRAYING IN THE ATLÉTICO PARANAENSE CHANGING ROOM BEFORE THE GAME, SANTOS, BRAZIL.

– ARTHUR ROWSE

YOU NEVER TIRE OF SEEING THE BALL HIT THE NET.

IPANEMA BEACH,
RIO DE JANEIRO, BRAZIL.

– KEVIN KEEGAN

›› **THE HOMELESS WORLD CUP, GOTHENBURG, SWEDEN.**

›››› **A HEERENVEEN FAN ARRIVES EARLY FOR A MATCH AGAINST RBC, HEERENVEEN, HOLLAND.**

LOVE IS FIRST, FOOTBALL
SECOND. MAYBE IT'S A
PHOTO FINISH.
– GIAMPIERO MASIERI

DUTHUNI, SOUTH AFRICA.

MY IDEA OF PARADISE IS A STRAIGHT LINE TO GOAL.
– FRIEDRICH NIETZSCHE

THE KHAYELITSHA TOWNSHIP, CAPE TOWN, SOUTH AFRICA.

›› OSLO, NORWAY.

›››› XINGU TRIBE OF THE NORTH EAST AMAZON, BRAZIL.

IT ONLY TAKES A SECOND TO SCORE A GOAL.
– BRIAN CLOUGH

CELEBRATIONS AFTER A GOAL
AT A RURAL VILLAGE,
LUNUNGWI, SOUTH AFRICA.

THE GOALKEEPER IS THE JEWEL IN THE CROWN, AND GETTING AT HIM SHOULD BE ALMOST IMPOSSIBLE.
– GEORGE GRAHAM

IF FOOTBALL IS AN ART, I WAS AN ARTIST.
– GEORGE BEST

A CHILD PLAYS ON HIS ROOF GARDEN ON AVENUE RIUS TAULET, BARCELONA, SPAIN.

›› SNOWFLAKES FC GIRLS' UNDER-9 TEAM IN FALGARWOOD, TORONTO, CANADA.

›››› CHEERLEADERS AT WOODLANDS STADIUM, SINGAPORE.

I LEARNED THAT THE BALL
NEVER CAME TO YOU WHERE
YOU EXPECTED IT. THIS HELPED
ME IN LIFE... EVERYTHING I'VE
LEARNED ABOUT
MORALITY AND DUTY
I OWE TO FOOTBALL.
– ALBERT CAMUS

**TEENAGERS WAIT FOR AN
IRELAND UNDER-21 MATCH TO
BEGIN, CORK, IRELAND.**

IN LATIN AMERICA, THE BORDER BETWEEN SOCCER AND POLITICS IS VAGUE. THERE'S A LONG LIST OF GOVERNMENTS THAT HAVE FALLEN OR BEEN OVERTHROWN AFTER THE DEFEAT OF THE NATIONAL TEAM. – LUIS SUAREZ

IF THERE IS NO FRIENDSHIP, THERE'S NO FOOTBALL.

STREET KIDS, PISAC, PERU. — FERENC PUSKAS

TO THINK OF FOOTBALL AS MERELY 22 HIRELINGS KICKING A BALL IS MERELY TO SAY THAT A VIOLIN IS WOOD AND CAT-GUT, HAMLET SO MUCH INK AND PAPER. IT IS CONFLICT AND ART. – J. B. PRIESTLEY

SMOKE FROM FLARES COVERS THE PITCH AFTER WILLEM II SCORE AGAINST AJAX, TILBURG, HOLLAND.

›› DEPORTIVO MUNICIPAL VERSUS VIRGEN DE CHAPI, LIMA, PERU.

›››› TWO YOUNG WOMEN WATCH THEIR FAVORITE PLAYERS CLOSELY DURING A CEREZO OSAKA FC TRAINING SESSION, OSAKA, JAPAN.

EVEN IF THERE WAS A HAND, IT WAS THE HAND OF GOD.

A YOUNG GIRL PLAYS WITH HER FATHER AT THE TEMPLE OF OLYMPIAN ZEUS, ATHENS, GREECE.

– DIEGO MARADONA

FOOTBALL IS A SIMPLE GAME; 22 MEN CHASE A BALL FOR 90 MINUTES AND AT THE END, THE GERMANS WIN. – GARY LINEKER

ENGLAND UNDER-21 CHANGING ROOM BEFORE A WORLD CUP QUALIFIER AGAINST AUSTRIA, LEEDS, ENGLAND.

»› GRASSROOTS FOOTBALL, OSLO, NORWAY.

»›› THE VILLAGE MATCH, LUNUNGWI, SOUTH AFRICA.

EACH SUCCEEDS IN REACHING THE GOAL BY A DIFFERENT METHOD.
– NICCOLÒ MACHIAVELLI

BLACK LEOPARDS FC TRAINING SESSION, MAKHADO, SOUTH AFRICA.

SANTOS FANS WATCH THEIR
TEAM LOSE AT VILA BELMIRO,
SANTOS, BRAZIL.

›› VANCOUVER WHITECAPS FC
VERSUS ATLANTA SILVER-
BACKS AT THE DEKALB
MEMORIAL STADIUM,
CLARKSTON, USA.

›››› WORKERS AT A BANANA
PLANTATION DURING A BREAK,
THOHOYANDOU, SOUTH AFRICA.

IT'S NOT JUST A SIMPLE GAME. IT IS A WEAPON OF THE REVOLUTION.
– CHE GUEVARA

303

FOOTBALL IS A PART OF I. WHEN I PLAY THE WORLD WAKES UP AROUND ME.
– BOB MARLEY

PLAYING AGAINST A DEFENSIVE OPPONENT IS AS BAD AS MAKING LOVE TO A TREE.
– JORGE VALDANO

MORIYAMAKITA HIGH SCHOOL, JAPAN.

THE BALL GAVE ME PRESTIGE, GAVE ME FAME, GAVE ME RICHES. THANK YOU, OLD FRIEND.
– ALFREDO DI STEFANO

AN EMPTY GOAL, BORACIA BEACH, SAO PAULO, BRAZIL.

›› JUNIOR FOOTBALL AT INGLEWOOD PARK, PERTH, AUSTRALIA.

›››› KIDS PLAYING IN JANDIA ON THE ISLAND OF FUERTEVEN- TURA, SPAIN.

A NATIONAL FOOTBALL TEAM REPRESENTS A WAY OF BEING, A CULTURE.
– MICHEL PLATINI

NIGHTTIME KICK-ABOUT IN RED SQUARE, MOSCOW, RUSSIA.

FOOTBALL IS MADE UP OF MISTAKES, BECAUSE A PERFECT MATCH IS 0-0.
– MICHEL PLATINI

THE GREAT FALLACY IS THAT THIS GAME IS FIRST AND LAST ABOUT WINNING. IT IS NOTHING OF THE KIND. THE GAME IS ABOUT GLORY; IT IS ABOUT DOING THINGS WITH STYLE.

– DANNY BLANCHFLOWER

MORROKA SWALLOWS PLAYERS DANCE AND SING ZULU SONGS BEFORE A GAME AGAINST THE KAISER CHIEFS, JOHANNESBURG, SOUTH AFRICA.

›› REFEREES TAKE A BREAK BETWEEN GAMES AT THE UMBRO INTERNATIONAL YOUTH CUP, MANCHESTER, ENGLAND.

›››› A SUPPORTER OF MOVERS FC OUTSIDE HIS HOUSE IN MOTSOALEDI, SOWETO, SOUTH AFRICA.

IN FOOTBALL, EVERYTHING IS COMPLICATED BY THE PRESENCE OF THE OPPOSITE TEAM. – JEAN-PAUL SARTRE

IRELAND VERSUS FRANCE AT
LANDSDOWNE ROAD, DUBLIN,
IRELAND.

›› AREQUIPA, PERU.

›››› CRESPO, AN IMMIGRANT
VILLAGE NEAR AREQUIPA,
PERU.

FOOTBALL WITHOUT FANS IS NOTHING.
– JOCK STEIN

YOUR ONLY SECURITY IN FOOTBALL SHOULD BE YOUR ABILITY.
– BILL NICHOLSON

BRAZIL'S FORWARD STRETCHES BEFORE THE SEMI-FINAL AT THE HOMELESS WORLD CUP, GOTHENBURG, SWEDEN.

FIVE DAYS SHALT THOU LABOR, THE BIBLE SAYS. THE SEVENTH DAY IS THE LORD THY GOD'S. THE SIXTH DAY IS FOR FOOTBALL.
— ANTHONY BURGESS

NUMBERS BEING PRINTED ONTO SHIRTS IN A HOTEL ROOM BEFORE AN ENGLAND UNDER-21 GAME, LEEDS, ENGLAND.

» A PUPIL OF THE SHANGHAI SHENUA FOOTBALL SCHOOL DURING AFTERNOON TRAINING, SHANGHAI, CHINA.

»»» SUPPORTER AT A J-LEAGUE GAME, JAPAN.

331

ALCOHOLISM V. COMMUNISM.
– SCOTTISH WORLD CUP BANNER V. USSR, 1982

IRISH SUPPORTERS PREPARE FOR A WORLD CUP QUALIFIER AGAINST FRANCE, DUBLIN, IRELAND.

FOOTBALL IS SUCH A FUNNY GAME. IT'S A FAIRY TALE REALLY. — ALEX FERGUSON

AN EMPTY GOAL IN THE NORTH OF NORWAY.

» SCHOOLCHILDREN PLAYING, MACHEKOANENG, LESOTHO.

»»» WOODLANDS WELLINGTON VERSUS BALESTIER KHALSA, SINGAPORE.

COLORFUL BRAZILIAN FOOTBALL, PUBLIC FLEXIBILITY AND ENJOYMENT, SURPRISE AND ELEGANCE. IT IS BOTH WISTFUL AND WILD. THE DANCE ON THE FIELD GIVES PEOPLE ECSTASY IN THE STADIUM AND JOY IN LIFE.
– GILBERTO FREYRE

FOOTBALL IS A SIMPLE GAME. THE HARD PART IS MAKING IT LOOK SIMPLE.

THE NORWAY CUP, OSLO, NORWAY.

– RON GREENWOOD

» CHILDREN PLAY IN FRONT OF THEIR HOUSE IN AN INFORMAL SETTLEMENT KNOWN AS MAKHASA 1 IN THE KHAYELITSHA TOWNSHIP OF CAPE TOWN, SOUTH AFRICA.

»»» MONWABISI PARK IN THE KHAYELITSHA TOWNSHIP OF CAPE TOWN, SOUTH AFRICA.

343

GOAL NUMBER 19 ON HACKNEY MARSHES IN EAST LONDON, ENGLAND. HACKNEY MARSHES HOLDS THE LARGEST CONCENTRATION OF FOOTBALL PITCHES IN EUROPE WITH A TOTAL OF 67 WORKING PITCHES.

THE MISSING OF CHANCES IS ONE OF THE MYSTERIES OF LIFE. – ALF RAMSEY

›› A BOCA JUNIORS FAN GESTURES TO RIVER PLATE FANS, BUENOS AIRES, ARGENTINA.

›››› UNDERNEATH THE STANDS ON MATCH NIGHT AT THE BLACK LEOPARDS' STADIUM, MAKHADO, SOUTH AFRICA.

THE 1970 WORLD CUP
WAS THE HIGH POINT OF THE
BRAZILIAN ART OF FOOTBALL.
I SPENT THE LAST FIFTEEN
MINUTES OF THE
FINAL AGAINST ITALY
(4-1) CRYING. – TOSTAO

BANPAKU MEMORIAL STADIUM,
SUITA, JAPAN.

>> AL MAFOOT FC, A SMALL
PRIVATELY-OWNED TEAM ON
THE BORDER OF DUBAI AND
OMAN.

>>>> SUNSET FOOTBALL,
HAMUTSHA, SOUTH AFRICA.

349

SOCCER IS THE BIGGEST THING THAT HAPPENED IN CREATION. IT'S BIGGER THAN ANY 'ISM' YOU CAN NAME. – ALAN BROWN

>> MINEOLA SC GIRLS' UNDER-9 TEAM TRAINS AT MINEOLA WILSON PARK, LONG ISLAND, USA.

>>>> FOOTBALL BEING PLAYED AT A JUNIOR SCHOOL PLAYGROUND, MAKHADO, SOUTH AFRICA.

IF GOD HAD MEANT US TO PLAY FOOTBALL IN THE SKY, HE'D HAVE PUT GRASS UP THERE. – BRIAN CLOUGH.

TEENAGERS PLAYING ON THE CRATER OF MOUNT EDEN, A DORMANT VOLCANO, AUCKLAND, NEW ZEALAND.

» **FOOTBALL AT SUNSET, LIMA, PERU.**

»»» **AFTER MAKING GOALPOSTS OF THEIR SKIS, TWO CHILDREN PLAY A GAME IN THE SNOW, GRUE, NORWAY.**

THEY SAID: "RIVELLINO'S CELEBRATIONS WERE MASTERPIECES OF MADNESS."

MAYBE BECAUSE A GOAL IS THE ULTIMATE IN FOOTBALL. WHEN YOU SCORE A GOAL, YOU LET LOOSE EVERYTHING WHICH IS INSIDE OF YOU. PELÉ ONCE COMPARED SCORING A GOAL TO AN ORGASM. IT DEPENDS ON THE GOALS, BUT YES IT CAN BE BETTER THAN SEX. – RIVELLINO

FOOTBALL IS A SIMPLE GAME FOR SIMPLE PEOPLE. BUT YOU ARE SUPPOSED TO PLAY IT INTELLIGENTLY!
– DIMITAR PENEV

SECURITY IS TIGHT DURING THE MOSCOW DERBY BETWEEN SPARTAK MOSCOW AND DINAMO MOSCOW, RUSSIA.

»» **BABYLON FAVELA, RIO DE JANEIRO, BRAZIL.**

»»» **BEACH SOCCER ON VIRGINIA BEACH, VIRGINIA, USA.**

THE GOALKEEPER IS THE LONE EAGLE, THE MAN OF MYSTERY, THE LAST DEFENDER. LESS THE KEEPER OF A GOAL THAN THE KEEPER OF A DREAM. – VLADIMIR NABAKOV

DEFENSIVE FOOTBALL IS LIKE A DICTATORSHIP. IT SUBJUGATES THE FREE SPIRIT. SO WE PLAYED WITH ARTISTRY. A VEILED PROTEST IN THE LANGUAGE OF FOOTBALL. IN TRIBUTE TO OUR OLD AND BELOVED ARGENTINA.

– CÉSAR LUIS MENOTTI

I WANT TO PLAY SEXY FOOTBALL. – RUUD GULLIT

**THE SPARTAK CROWD
ERUPTS AFTER THE
WINNING GOAL AGAINST
DINAMO MOSCOW, RUSSIA.**

›› PARIS, FRANCE.

**›››› SUNSET FOOTBALL
ON LEGIAN BEACH, BALI,
INDONESIA.**

376

ONE DAY A WOMAN WILL APPEAR WHO

IS FAST AND STRONG AND CAN MAKE A BALL SPIN INTO WHICHEVER PART OF THE BACK OF THE NET SHE CHOOSES... THAT WOMAN WILL NOT BE ME. BUT I DOUBT HER JOY WILL BE ANY MORE INTENSE THAN THE HAPPINESS I FEEL WHEN I AM JUST ABOUT ACCEPTABLE ON THE SOCCER FIELD. – ALYSON RUDD

BASICALLY, IT'S ALL FOOTBALL.
– JACK CHARLTON

PHOTOGRAPHY Levon Biss | **QUOTES** compiled by Jacob Lehman and Raf Willems | **CAPTIONS** Levon Biss, RPM London | **ENGLISH TRANSLATION** Dice Vertalingen | **LAYOUT** Studio Lannoo | **PRINTED AND BOUND BY** Proost Printers, Turnhout, Belgium
WITH SPECIAL THANKS TO Colin Henry – UMBRO International Ltd; Paul Nugent – UMBRO International Ltd; Victoria Atherstone – RPM London; Lee Farrant – RPM London; Justine Norman, RPM London, UMBRO's global licensee network and Apple Computer Inc.
Steve Rushin is a senior writer for *Sports Illustrated* magazine and was voted 2005 National Sportswriter of the Year by the National Sportswriters and Sportscasters Association.
PHOTO P. 2 Ground staff at CD Espanyol give the grass one final cut before the game, Barcelona, Spain.
PHOTO P. 6 Shanghai Shenua FC fans celebrate victory in the final game of the season, Shanghai, China.

This edition first published in the United States of America in 2006 by Universe Publishing
A Division of Rizzoli International Publications, Inc., 300 Park Avenue South, New York, NY 10010

2006 2007 2008 | 10 9 8 7 6 5 4 3 2 1
ISBN-13: 978-0-7893-1510-6 | ISBN-10: 0-7893-1510-6
Library of Congress Control Number: 2006901450
www.levonbiss.com | www.rpmphotos.com | www.umbro.com | www.lannoo.com | www.rizzoliusa.com